Orthodoxy for Children

**Fr. Anthony Borisov**

# Confession

**Illustrations by
Natalia Lobanova**

Grand Rapids · Exaltation Press · 2019

Copyright © 2019 Exaltation Press

Author: Fr. Anthony Borisov
Illustrator: Natalia Lobanova
Translator: Fr. John Hogg

"Confession"
This book is designed to help children understand the purpose of Holy Confession in the Orthodox Church, beginning by introducing them to the conscience, the idea of right and wrong, and then explaining the purpose and practicalities of Confession.

All rights reserved. This book or any portion thereof may not be reproduced or used in any manner whatsoever without the express written permission of the publisher except for the use of brief quotations in a book review.

Translated from the original "Об исповеди" by Nikea Press, Copyright © Trading house «NIKEA», www.Nikeabooks.ru

ISBN: 978-1-950067-51-0 (Paperback)

Edited by Cynthia Hogg

First printing edition 2019

Exaltation Press
Grand Rapids, MI

www.ExaltationPress.com

For bulk orders, please contact editor@exaltationpress.com.

# Table of Contents

WHEN DOES YOUR CONSCIENCE SPEAK? .................................................................. 4
THE CONSCIENCE - THE VOICE OF GOD .................................................................. 6
WHAT IS SIN? .................................................................................................................. 8
WHEN DID EVIL FIRST APPEAR? .................................................................................. 10
THE GRIEF OF THE OLD TESTAMENT AND THE WORK OF CHRIST .................... 12
WHAT IS CONFESSION? ................................................................................................ 14
HOW CONFESSION CAME INTO BEING ...................................................................... 16
MY FIRST CONFESSION ................................................................................................ 18
HOW OFTEN SHOULD YOU GO TO CONFESSION? .................................................. 20
WHY DO WE NEED A PRIEST FOR CONFESSION? .................................................. 22
WHY ARE THERE A CROSS AND GOSPEL BOOK ON THE TABLE AT CONFESSION? ................................................................................................................ 24
THE SEAL OF CONFESSION ........................................................................................ 26
DO NOT JUDGE OTHERS ............................................................................................ 28
WHEN DOES GOD NOT HEAR OUR CONFESSION? ................................................ 30
WHAT IS REPENTANCE? .............................................................................................. 32

## WHEN DOES YOUR CONSCIENCE SPEAK?

I wonder... Do you know what your conscience is? Often, people find out what their conscience is fairly early on. I remember hearing my conscience when I was five years old. It spoke to me after I took something that didn't belong to me without asking. It was a toy. I really liked it but it belonged to a different little boy. When no one was watching, I took it without permission. At first, I was happy. Suddenly, though, the happiness disappeared and I heard a voice inside myself. The voice was both mine and not mine at the same time. The voice was strict but kind. It told me that I had made a mistake and that if I kept acting that way, all my joy would disappear. I was frightened and so I gave the toy back to the boy it belonged to and I asked his forgiveness. Then, the voice grew quiet. That voice was my conscience.

> "Better paint on my face than a stain in my heart."
>
> Miguel Cervantes, Spanish writer

5 Confession

# THE CONSCIENCE - THE VOICE OF GOD

Once I had heard my conscience, I began to wonder. Who did that voice belong to? Could it be that I was reproaching myself like that? Probably not. After all, the toy was nice and I really liked it. So what if it didn't belong to me? When I took it, I should have been glad but instead felt only disappointment. There must have been someone talking to me who cared if what I did was good or bad. That person was warning me not to hurt or do wrong to others. Someone was disappointed to see me steal something and decided to help me. My parents often did that but they weren't there to see when I took the toy. Who, then, sees everything?

> "What exactly is the conscience? The conscience is the quiet voice of God, felt by each of us in our hearts."
>
> *St. Luke of Crimea*

When I thought about it, I realized it was God. It was His voice that I heard inside myself. God attentively watches us and tries to keep each of us from making mistakes.

Two people were riding in a cart. They saw a haystack. One of them decided to steal the hay and said to the other, "I'll take the hay and if you notice anyone watching, give me a signal." He took a big armful of hay and started to run back. His friend started waving at him as if he had noticed someone. The thief was frightened and threw the hay back and looked around. He didn't see anyone. He got angry with his friend and asked, "Who saw me trying to steal the hay?" "God saw," his friend answered. "He sees everything and nothing is hidden from His eyes."

# WHAT IS SIN?

Have you ever been sick? Did you have a cough, a stuffy nose, or a fever? It doesn't feel very good, does it? Sin is also a sickness, not of body, but of soul. When we do something wrong, when we go against our conscience, against God, we begin to be sick. It is like our soul is crying. Joy leaves our life and we cannot find any peace. Our conscience points to our mistake, to the evil that we have done.

### God is Merciful

Once, God appeared to an old woman in a village. She told the priest of the village Church what had happened. The priest told her, "If the Lord appears to you again, ask Him to tell you my sins since only He knows them. That will prove that it was really the Lord who appeared to you." After a little while, the old woman went back to the priest and said, "God appeared to me again." The priest asked, "Did you ask Him my question?" "Yes, I asked Him. He said, 'Tell your priest that I have forgotten his sins.'" "Then it truly was God!" the priest answered.

> "There is nothing bad inside mankind except sin. When sin has been destroyed, everything becomes light, easy, and peaceful."
>
> *St. John Chrysostom*

# Confession

## WHEN DID EVIL FIRST APPEAR?

There hasn't always been evil in the world. There was a time when evil didn't even exist. When God created mankind, He wanted us always to be like Him. God is the kindest, most honest, and most caring. At first, Adam and Eve, the first human beings, were just like that, too. Unfortunately, they later changed. God placed Adam and Eve in the most beautiful place, the garden of Paradise. There, He spoke to them directly. God allowed them to eat the fruit of many different trees. There was only one tree that He asked them not to touch. It wasn't that the tree was bad. God wanted Adam and Eve to do as He asked so that, by loving what was good, they would grow and become more self sufficient. The first human beings, though, did not act as God had hoped. They did not do as God had instructed and they tasted the fruit of the forbidden tree. By itself, this mistake wasn't so bad. What was worse was something else. They tried to lie to God, their Creator. Then, evil began to live inside them. And what is evil and sinful cannot live comfortably in the presence of God.

11 Confession

# THE GRIEF OF THE OLD TESTAMENT AND THE WORK OF CHRIST

Adam and Eve longed to return to the garden of Paradise but were not able to. Because of their sinful actions, they were no longer able to talk to God directly. The children of Adam and Eve and all of their descendants after them lived with the dream of someday returning to Paradise. Their dream was fulfilled when Mary, the Theotokos, gave birth to the Savior of the world, Jesus Christ. Christ taught us how to be good.

Christ is the Son of God. He came into the world to save mankind and to bring us back to Paradise. Of course, it was no longer the same garden of Paradise where Adam and Eve had lived but rather, somewhere even more amazing - the Kingdom of Heaven. While you cannot see it with your eyes, God's Kingdom exists even now. All those who believe in God and live with a clean conscience can enter it.

> "God is very near to us but high above us at the same time. In order for someone to 'incline' God to come down and abide with him, he must humble himself and repent. Then, the Most-merciful God, seeing his humility, will raise him to the Heavens and love him with a great love."
>
> *Venerable Paisius of Mt. Athos*

# Confession

## WHAT IS CONFESSION?

Confession is one of the Mysteries of the Church. In Confession, God forgives us our sins. Why do we need Confession? Do you remember how we said that sin is a sickness? When we do something wrong, our soul gets sick. It doesn't feel well. Sin, just like bacteria or a virus, makes our souls suffer. If we get a cold, we take medicine. If we sin, we need to go to Confession. In Confession, God treats our souls. That is why the Mystery of Confession is often called "a spiritual hospital." How is God able to deliver us from sin? It is hard to understand completely. There's a reason why Confession is called one of the "Mysteries." We can, however, say this much about Confession. When we repent of our sins in Confession, God, seeing our desire to overcome them, helps us to get rid of them. Have you ever had a splinter? Even though it's just a little piece of wood, a splinter really hurts when it gets under our skin and it can be difficult to get rid of it without the help of a grown-up. In the same way, in Confession, God takes away sin like a splinter. We cannot pull it out by ourselves. God helps us.

---

**The Joy of Repentance**

Someone came to Confession. There was a long line, perhaps an hour or two, if not more. "Should I just leave?" he thought. However, the voice of his conscience said, "Be patient for an hour or two and repent of your sins. Then you'll see that you did the right thing." The man stayed in the Church. After Confession, his conscience asked him, "Do you feel better now?" "There's nothing better!" the man said joyfully. "Yes, there is!" his conscience answered. "Keep this purity of heart and you will enter Paradise. It is even more joyful there. And that joy never leaves you."

"There is no sin that cannot be corrected through repentance."
St. John Chrysostom

"No sin is unforgivable except a sin that we do not repent of."
Venerable Isaac the Syrian

# HOW CONFESSION CAME INTO BEING

The Kingdom of God is a place where only good and honest people may live. There is no place there for evil, envy, or cruelty. The Lord really wants human beings to be like Him. He wants us to treat others with sincere love, to care for those around us and not to live just for ourselves. I'm sure that's exactly how you try to live. But sometimes, even good and kind people make mistakes. Just like Adam and Eve.

What can you do when sin has entered your life? That was a question that Christians were already asking two thousand years

### The Parable of the Prodigal Son

A son asked his father to give him the part of the inheritance that was set aside for him. When he received the money, the young man set out for a different country, where he quickly wasted all of his father's money and became poor. Suffering and in need, the young man realized that he had gone astray and that only his loving father could help him. The prodigal son decided to return home. As soon as the father heard that his son was coming home, he ran out himself to meet him, embraced him, and forgave him everything. God also forgives us our sins each and every time that we turn away from them.

ago. That was when Confession first appeared. Back then, it was a lot different than how it is now. Today, we tell our sins only to the priest. The first Christians, however, confessed their sins publicly, in the presence of many other Christians. Over time, that kind of Confession was no longer used.

## MY FIRST CONFESSION

Every adult used to be a child. I was once a child, too. I remember that I thought my life was very interesting. After all, I had a secret that I hardly ever told anyone about. I'll tell it to you, though: I went to Church. Usually, I'd go with my mom or my grandmother. Everything in the Church seemed familiar to me – the icons, the candles, the singing of the choir, the wooden bench that I always wanted to sit on the corner of. I also knew the old priest that served our parish. It always seemed to me that the priest saw a little bit more than the other people and knew more.

Once, the day arrived when I had to talk to the priest one-on-one. I had just turned seven and my grandmother told me, "Now, you'll go to Confession!" I knew that Confession was when you had to go to the priest and tell him something. But what did you tell him? That I didn't yet know. I asked my grandmother. In a stern voice, but with a smile, she told me, "Tell him what your conscience tells you to." I remember telling the priest about my mistakes in a voice so quiet you could barely hear it. To my great relief, he didn't lecture me but just covered my head with some kind of fabric and quietly said the words of a prayer. That prayer made my soul feel very light and easy.

> "Open your conscience before God, show Him your wounds, and ask Him to give you medicine. Show yourself to the One who does not reproach but heals, for He sees everything, even if you keep quiet."
>
> *St. John Chrysostom*

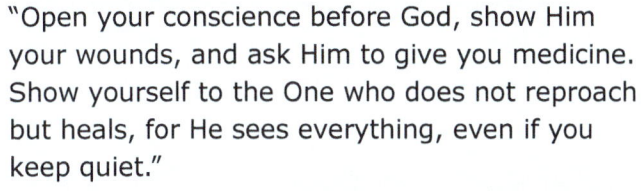

## HOW OFTEN SHOULD YOU GO TO CONFESSION?

This isn't an easy question to answer. All of us are different and have different personalities and each of us has our own path to God. Because of that, we can't make the same rules for everyone. We can't say, for example, that everyone has to confess once a month. The most important thing is to follow your conscience. Keep your conscience pure and listen to it. If your conscience tells you that you did something wrong, you should go to Confession. Some places require Confession each time you go to Communion and we should follow the rules of our particular parish. So if that's the case, what should you do if, for example, you are preparing yourself for Communion and your conscience is silent? What if you have behaved well and attentively followed what your conscience tells you and you can't remember offending anyone? Good job! But there's a problem. You have nothing to say in Confession but have to confess before going to Communion. If that's the case, go to the priest and tell him that you have tried to do your best and your conscience is quiet. The priest, seeing that you are obedient, will rejoice and let you go to Communion.

"Remember your sins before God if you wish for them to be forgiven and do not repay evil for evil to your neighbor."

*Abba Isaiah*

## WHY DO WE NEED A PRIEST FOR CONFESSION?

I know some adults who are afraid to go to Confession. In that way, they are a lot like children. Do you know why? It is because they are afraid of telling their sins to the priest. Sometimes, adults don't even understand – why do we even need the priest for Confession? I'll tell you why we need him. It's easy to admit your mistakes to yourself or to God who you cannot see. It is much harder to do that in the presence of another person, the priest. We inevitably feel ashamed for the mistakes we have made.

That shame is a lot like fire. It burns. Fire destroys some things but other things it makes better. For example, we know that gold is purified by fire. In that same way, in Confession, that shame helps to purify our soul. In Confession, we aren't telling our sins to the priest, but telling them to God in the presence of the priest. God hears our Confession. He is the one who forgives us our sins, not the priest. The grace of God works through the priest, in particular, when the priest puts his epitrachelion on our heads at the end of Confession and says the prayer of absolution.

**An Epitrachelion** (*from the Greek, meaning "something that goes around the neck"*) is a part of the vestments of an Orthodox priest. The epitrachelion is a symbol of the grace that is given to the priest. A priest cannot serve the Divine Services without an epitrachelion.

## WHY ARE THERE A CROSS AND GOSPEL BOOK ON THE TABLE AT CONFESSION?

The priest witnesses our Confession. How can we remember, however, that God also hears us when we express sorrow for our sins? To keep us from doubting, a tradition has developed. When you confess, a cross and a book of the Gospels are put on a special stand (an analogion). There is a reason for that. The Gospel (which is a marvelous book) describes the life and teachings of the Savior of the world, Jesus Christ. On the Cross, Christ accepted death for all people. Through His sacrifice, the Kingdom of Heaven was opened for all of us. The cross and the Gospel book are a direct reminder that God hears our Confession.

> "Behold, my child, Christ stands here invisibly receiving your Confession. Do not be ashamed or afraid and do not hide anything from me but without flinching, open to me everything that you have done and you will receive forgiveness from our Lord Jesus Christ. Here is His icon before us. I am only His witness, to testify before Him about everything that you tell me. If you hide your sin, you will fall into a double sin. Be attentive, therefore, for you have come to the hospital of your soul. Do not leave without being healed."
>
> *The exhortation of the priest before Confession*

After the priest says the prayer of absolution, we kiss the cross and Gospel. That has two meanings. First, it means that we are giving God thanks for forgiving us our sins. Second, it shows that we are making a promise to try not to repeat those sinful mistakes again.

## THE SEAL OF CONFESSION

For some reason, adults often think children are silly. Sometimes, however, they themselves believe silly things. Some people, for example, don't want to go to Confession because they're afraid everyone will find out about their mistakes. I'll tell you a secret, though. That's impossible! The priest, you see, has to keep the seal of Confession. He cannot tell anyone what he hears in Confession, even the people closest to him. Not even in a whisper. Before becoming a priest, he had to make a vow, a very big one. Among other things, a future priest vows to keep what is confessed to him secret. If he breaks that vow, he is forbidden to serve for three years. By the way, not even the government can force a priest to reveal what someone says in Confession. I'll tell you something else. Many priests even have bad memories for the sins of other people. They have their own sins to struggle against.

---

The Seal of Confession is "a divine secret, sealed with the seal of God Himself. No one is allowed to open that seal."

*St. Dimitri of Rostov*

# Confession

## DO NOT JUDGE OTHERS

I think by now you understand how to confess properly. A proper Confession is one in which we ask God sincerely to forgive us our sinful mistakes. We don't do this out of fear that He will punish us. We do it because we do not want to fall away from Him. The Lord is the source of joy and light. Sin takes all that away from us.

Now let's talk about what we should never do in Confession. Sometimes, when we go to Confession, we suddenly want to make excuses for ourselves. We want to make our sin seem a little smaller. Unfortunately, when we do that, the sin only gets worse.

More often than not, when we make excuses, we begin to shift our responsibility onto other people. We say something like, "Yes, of course, what I did was wrong, but somebody else pushed me into it." When we do that, instead of being set free from one sin, we commit another sin, the sin of judging others.

> When Christ was led to Golgotha, they crucified Him with thieves, one on His right side and one on His left. One of the evildoers who was crucified with Him mocked Him and said, "If you are the Christ, save yourself and us!" The other thief, however, rebuked him and said, "Do you not fear God? For you yourself are condemned for your wicked deeds! We are condemned justly but this Man has done nothing wrong!" Then, he said to Jesus, "Remember me, O Lord, when You come in Your Kingdom." Jesus said to him, "Truly I say to you, today you will be with me in Paradise."

## The Generous Merchant

There was a merchant. He went from village to village selling his wares. If someone didn't have money to pay, the merchant would loan him the money. "Look, I'm writing your name in this book. When I return, you'll pay me back." If the person still couldn't pay the next time, the merchant said sternly, "You can't pay me again, so I'm putting a cross next to your name in my book. I remember your debt. Next time, you have to pay me." If the debtor still didn't have the money the next time, the merchant spoke to him even more sternly and put another cross by his name. The third time, he would say, "Okay, I forgive your debt. I'm crossing out your name and the little crosses. The Lord is your judge, not me." Even though that merchant forgave people their debts, he never grew poor.

## WHEN DOES GOD NOT HEAR OUR CONFESSION?

It sometimes happens that God does not hear someone's Confession. Or rather, He hears that words are being said but does not accept them. This sad situation happens for one particular reason. It happens when we are upset with someone else and refuse to forgive them.

Just imagine for a moment: we come to God and ask Him to forgive us our sins. We, however, don't do what we ask Him to do. We keep bad feelings in our hearts. Remember, nothing that is bad or evil can ever feel comfortable in God's presence. If we ourselves don't forgive someone, it's as if we aren't actually asking God for forgiveness and there is no way for us to receive it. That isn't because God is hard or strict but rather because a heart that is filled with resentment is unable to let go of the splinter of sin. A heart like that is like a porcupine, with quills sticking out in all directions, not allowing God to touch it.

# 31 Confession

> "We must not blame our birth or any other person for our sins, but only ourselves."
>
> *Venerable Anthony the Great*

## WHAT IS REPENTANCE?

> "Sin is a wound and repentance is the medicine."
>
> *St. John Chrysostom*
>
> The Apostle Peter gave us a wonderful example of repentance. When Christ was arrested, Peter was afraid and denied Him three times. That betrayal weighed heavily on his conscience. He repented bitterly and tried to show his faithfulness to Christ with his actions. The Savior appeared to Peter and forgave him. Even such a serious sin can be forgiven, if someone sincerely repents and makes a firm decision never to repeat it again.

I remember how whenever I went to Confession, my grandmother loved to smile and ask me, "Well? Did you repent?" For a long time, I thought that Confession and repentance were the same thing. But that's not exactly true. Confession is when we say what our sins are, admitting them, and feeling contrition for them. Repentance is the fruit of true Confession. Do you know what the Orthodox Greeks call repentance? "A changing of the mind." That means that in Confession, we need to do more than just say what our sins are. We need to leave them behind, to try not to return to them. If you sincerely desire to do that, God will surely give you the strength to have "a change of mind," to change your life for the better, so that you can always be in harmony with your conscience and live with joy in your soul.